FIFTY MODERN BUILDINGS THAT CHANGED THE WORLD

DESIGN
MUSEUM

FIFTY MODERN BUILDINGS

THAT CHANGED THE WORLD

**DEYAN
SUDJIC**

conran
OCTOPUS

FIFTY MODERN BUILDINGS

FIFTY
MODERN
BUILDINGS

To design a building is to make a self-conscious prediction about the future while simultaneously, and often unknowingly, helping to define the past. Predictions about how buildings will be used, and what they will mean, made by those who commission them, as well as by those who go on to design them, are fascinating, revealing and almost always wrong. A forensic look at the indelible traces of history that a building contains within it, despite itself and despite its creators, is more telling.

Architects always struggle to shape buildings that reflect their dreams and ambitions, and sometimes those of their clients and patrons, too. Winston Churchill's version of this process was that we shape our buildings, and then they shape us. More often, it is events that intervene. Monuments built to celebrate national identity are co-opted and recycled by other nations – in the way that the parliament building in Dhaka built by Louis Kahn went from being a sign of West Pakistan's dominance in what was once East Pakistan, to become the national symbol of a newly independent Bangladesh.

The often intricate stories of how buildings come about, how they are built, adapted and transformed, give us an insight like no other into the shaping of our times. Taken together, they provide not just an account of the individual histories of a sequence of remarkable buildings, but an alternative history of the present.

Beijing's Olympic Stadium – the product of a collaboration between its architects and the artist Ai Weiwei – was conceived by the Chinese government as a national landmark, but who knows what its future symbolism will be?

THE CRYSTAL PALACE
London

1851
Joseph Paxton

Henry Cole, a civil servant with a passion for design, convinced Queen Victoria's consort, Prince Albert, to support the Great Exhibition. The exhibition itself was an astonishing assertion of Britain's industrial creativity at the height of its empire, but it was the building in which the exhibition was housed, rather than its contents, that was truly remarkable. Initially viewed with suspicion, both event and building – sited in London's Hyde Park – turned out to be a hugely popular success, despite the disapproval of the Arts & Crafts designer William Morris, who refused to set foot inside.

Designed by Joseph Paxton (1803–65) after an architectural competition failed to elicit anything that matched the ambition of the project, the Crystal Palace was a marvel of prefabrication. Paxton drew on his previous experience building greenhouses for the Duke of Devonshire at Chatsworth to design a structure almost 600 metres (2,000 ft) long and covering some 92,000 square metres (990,000 sq. ft). Paxton devised an ingenious cast-iron, timber and glass structure that had no architectural precedents. A specially designed trolley was used to speed up the installation of the glazing, and the palace took just eight months to build.

When the exhibition ended, the Crystal Palace was dismantled and moved across London to be re-erected in the south London suburb of Sydenham. Even though the palace itself was destroyed by fire in 1936, it is a project that has haunted the imagination of architects ever since. It inspired a not very faithful reconstruction in Texas and was a model for the mall at the World Financial Center in Manhattan. An example of organized and industrialized architecture, the Crystal Palace has been claimed by the high-tech architects of the 1980s, especially Norman Foster and Richard Rogers, as providing a precedent for their work.

It took just nine months from Joseph Paxton's first sketch to complete the Crystal Palace. In total, it attracted more than six million visitors, and even managed to make a profit.

THE CRYSTAL PALACE AT SYDENHAM.

No. 9.

GARDEN FRONT OF THE GREAT CENTRAL TRANSEPT.

London: Published by Read & Co., 15, Johnson's Court, Fleet Street.

AUSTRIAN POSTAL SAVINGS BANK
Vienna

At the start of the 20th century, the Austro-Hungarian Empire, of which Vienna was the capital, had less than 20 years left to live. But Vienna didn't look anything like a city in decline. It was growing fast: it had recently demolished the fortifications that encircled it and replaced them with the monumental and – it must be said – pompous Ringstrasse. And in Otto Wagner (1841–1918) it had an extraordinarily accomplished architect, who was also a gifted teacher and theorist. In 1894 he became Professor of Architecture at the Academy of Fine Arts, where, among others, he taught Josef Hoffmann and Joze Plecnik. Significantly, his inaugural address at the academy, subsequently published as a book, was entitled *Modern Architecture*. Three years later, Karl Lueger became the mayor of Vienna and set to work on a wholesale remodelling of the city. Wagner designed bridges, embankments and canals, and was also responsible for a couple of exquisite metro stations and a complex of psychiatric hospitals on the edge of the city.

Perhaps the most impressive of all his buildings was the Austrian Postal Savings Bank (Österreichische Postsparkasse), which was set back from the Ringstrasse, facing the vapid Ministry of War across an open square. Wagner designed every detail, from the aluminium maidens holding laurel wreaths aloft on the roof line to the furniture in the banking hall.

The Postal Savings Bank has a strong case for being considered one of the first monuments of modern architecture, in its use of new materials and in its revelation of the outer wall as no more than a screen, rather than as a massive load-carrying structure. The aluminium studs imply that the marble tiles are simply pinned in place, thus creating the first explicit curtain wall. Inside the banking hall is a milky glass vault, with ventilation provided by free-standing, exposed tubular ducts.

Otto Wagner designed every detail of the bank: the chairs, with their protective metal socks to guard their legs, the clocks and the light fittings. He was eager to demonstrate the decorative possibilities of modern materials.

GOLDMAN & SALATSCH BUILDING
Vienna

Adolf Loos (1870–1933) made an impact as much as a polemicist as for the restricted number of buildings that he actually completed. He was acerbic in his onslaught on the Wiener Werkstätte, the design workshops started by his contemporary and rival Josef Hoffmann, which he suggested existed solely to make work for underemployed wealthy young women, as well as on self-consciously 'artistic' architecture. His famous 1910 lecture 'Ornament and Crime' (published 1913) was a reflection on an architecture of aristocratic restraint, in which the inherent qualities of materials provided richness enough without the application of any further decoration. Loos believed in careful proportions and handsome spaces.

Although he preached discretion, Loos relished, even encouraged, the notoriety that his project for the gentlemen's outfitters Goldman & Salatsch attracted. The store occupied a prominent corner site on Michaelerplatz, immediately behind one of the entrances to the Hofburg Palace, the winter residence of the Austrian emperor. It was one of a number of projects that Loos designed for fashion industry clients, which also included two branches of the menswear store Knize. When the design was unveiled, its façades, stripped of any applied classical architectural detail, were mocked. A cartoonist suggested that Loos's inspiration for the main elevation came from a drain cover. One newspaper called it a 'dung heap'; another decried it as looking like a grain elevator next to the Hofburg Palace.

Unabashed, Loos defended his design in a series of public lectures. But Vienna's town council refused to grant a permit of occupation until Loos compromised to the extent of applying window boxes to the façade.

Adolf Loos was an enthusiastic polemicist, ready to defend his most controversial work against the abuse of Vienna's newspapers with a series of public lectures.

AKADEMISCHER VERBAND FÜR LITERATUR U. MUSIK

MOTTO: "EIN SCHEUSAL VON EINEM HAUS" (AUS EINER WIENER GEMEINDERATSSITZUNG)

IM SOPHIENSAAL

MONTAG, DEN 11. DEZEMBER 1911 UM HALB 8 UHR
ABENDS VORTRAG DES ARCHITEKTEN ADOLF LOOS

MEIN · HAUS · AM
MICHAELERPLATZ

MIT SKIOPTIKONBILDERN

Karten bei Kehlendorfer I, Krugerstr. 3 zu K 4, 3, 2, 1, —.50

Mitglieder des „Akademischen Verbandes für Literatur und Musik in Wien" und des „Vereines
für Kunst und Kultur" zahlen halben Preis · Die Mitgliederaufnahme erfolgt tägl. von 10—12 Uhr
vormittags im Hause I. Bezirk, Reichsratsstrasse 7

MONUMENT TO THE THIRD INTERNATIONAL

1919
(conceived, unbuilt)
Vladimir Tatlin

Vladimir Tatlin (1885–1953), alongside Kazimir Malevich, was the key figure in the Soviet avant-garde in the years after the 1917 Russian Revolution. He was a significant painter and sculptor. He also designed rationalized 'workers clothing' and furniture, and explored the idea of flying machines. He survived the Stalinist purges, but never succeeded in realizing an architectural project.

His key work, the Monument to the Third International, conceived in 1919, flickers on the edge of reality. It was a project that a country shattered by war and civil war, as the Soviet Union had been, could never have built. Even if the Soviet Union had had the resources, the design itself stretched the limits of the possible: it was intended to rise higher than the Eiffel Tower. Tatlin designed it to contain three Platonic forms – a cube, a pyramid and a cylinder – which would rotate at different speeds within its spiralling structure.

It was also an intensely political project. The Third International (an organisation of national communist parties) was brought into being by Lenin in 1915 in opposition to the Second Socialist International, the congress of left-wing parties from across Europe that was prepared either to support their national governments in World War I or take a pacifist position. In 1919 Lenin convened the Third International in Moscow to consolidate the power of his party, to set the model for smaller national communist parties and to expel socialists and pacifists. Tatlin's monument was intended to house a permanent base for the organization, and had a scale and architectural language to match Lenin's ambitions.

'Tatlin's Tower' has been continually celebrated in exhibitions of the art and design of the period, built as smaller replicas – most recently in the courtyard of the Royal Academy in London, and before that at the Hayward Gallery, also in London, and at the Centre Pompidou in Paris.

In the midst of the turmoil of a revolution and a civil war, the closest that Tatlin got to realizing his vision was a wood and plaster model built in his studio. His project has remained a ghostlike presence, continually recreated on a miniature scale for museums.

LINGOTTO
FIAT FACTORY
Turin

1923
Giacomo Mattè-Trucco

Fiat's Lingotto complex was an extraordinary summation of the factory architecture of its time, running straight as an engineer could make it for more than a third of a kilometre, and topped by a rooftop test track with spiral concrete access ramps at either end. It looked as if it owed more to the overheated rhetoric of Futurism than to pragmatic business sense, yet it was the cornerstone of Italy's capitalist economy.

By learning from Henry Ford's Detroit, the Agnelli family created one of Europe's great dynastic businesses. Ford himself had borrowed the meat-packing techniques of Chicago's slaughterhouses, and used them to build automobiles quickly, efficiently and cheaply, moving half-finished car bodies slung from chains on a production line, like carcasses. In so doing, he invented the 20th-century factory.

No cars have been made at Lingotto for 40 years. It is a hotel, shop and office complex now. Perched on the roof is the art gallery that houses Gianni Agnelli's art collection, and where he lay in state on his death.

Under the rigorous neoclassical façades of the Fiat factory is a reinforced concrete structure. Most innovative of all was the test track on the roof, which captured the imagination of Le Corbusier.

BAUHAUS
Dessau

1925–26
Walter Gropius

The first of the three homes that the Bauhaus occupied in its short life was an existing art school in Weimar. The last was a redundant factory in Berlin. But the school's lasting fame comes from the Dessau building that Walter Gropius (1883–1969) designed in 1925, and inaugurated in 1926.

Dessau, a small town not far from Berlin, had an ambitious mayor who was so eager to attract the Bauhaus that he was ready to pay for a new building containing studios, workshops, a lecture theatre, canteen and student dormitories on a site on the edge of the town. In addition, on a second site there were houses for the 'Masters' – one accommodated Gropius himself; Wassily Kandinsky had another. The scale of its all-glass studio walls, the dynamic pinwheel plan and the cantilevered balconies defined the heroic period of modernism. The idea of placing a studio on a bridge between the two main blocks was another bravura gesture.

Gropius's reputation today is greater as an educator than it is as an architect, but the Bauhaus at Dessau – his most accomplished building and the embodiment of the 'International Style', as identified by Philip Johnson and Henry-Russell Hitchcock in the 1932 exhibition they staged for the Museum of Modern Art in New York – is one of the few buildings that can be said to have defined its times. It was a built manifesto for the functionalist ethos of the Bauhaus approach to design.

In 1932 a right-wing city administration evicted the Bauhaus, then under the directorship of Mies van der Rohe, and the Nazis called for what they described as a 'cathedral of Bolshevism' to be demolished, or at least 'Aryanized', which meant adding a pitched roof. After the Bauhaus moved out, the building was used by the Junkers aircraft company, with the chief test pilot taking over Kandinsky's house. Both the school and the Masters' houses were badly damaged in the last days of the second World War, unsympathetically restored afterwards by the East Germans, and more carefully a second time by the Bauhaus Foundation and, in 1996, the Bauhaus Dessau was declared a World Heritage site.

In its restored form, the Dessau Bauhaus reflects its appearance in Walter Gropius's time. The damage inflicted by wartime bombing, and unsympathetic alterations during both the Nazi and the East German periods have been erased.

GERMAN PAVILION
Barcelona

1929
Ludwig Mies
van der Rohe

National pavilions at World Fairs are rarely intended to become permanent buildings. That of Weimar Germany at the Barcelona International Exposition of 1929 was no exception. Even though it was the encapsulation of all that Ludwig Mies van der Rohe (1886–1969) believed in, contained within just 1,000 square metres (10,800 sq. ft), it was dismantled when the fair closed. According to legend, fragments of travertine and onyx were transported across the border to be dumped in France, so avoiding import duties.

The exquisite pavilion became a fading memory, with little more than the photographs of Mies in his silk top hat at the opening ceremony left as a record. The most tangible reminder that it had existed was the Barcelona chair, the piece of furniture that Mies had designed specifically for the pavilion. At the opening ceremony, the King and Queen of Spain used the chairs as thrones. The German commissioner's speech explained: 'We wished here to show what we can do, what we are, how we feel today and see. We do not want anything but clarity, simplicity and honesty.'

The pavilion was flanked by a series of exhibition halls showcasing German industrial production, designed by Mies's lover, Lilly Reich. But in the pavilion itself there was almost nothing to see but architecture: travertine floors and marble walls, two rows of chrome-plated, cruciform steel columns, green glass and a reflecting pool, with a single figure sculpted by Georg Kolbe. In Barcelona's design-led, post-Franco revival in the 1980s, Cristian Cirici was commissioned to reconstruct the pavilion on its original site on the edge of Montjuic Park.

With nothing much more than fragments of sketches to work with, Cristian Cirici undertook exhaustive research to get his reconstruction of Ludwig Mies van der Rohe's lost masterpiece right, even down to finding stone from the original quarries.

VILLA SAVOYE
Poissy

1931
Le Corbusier

Originally named Les Heures Claires, the villa is now known as the Savoye, after Pierre Savoye, the wealthy businessman who commissioned it as a weekend retreat in Poissy, around 30 kilometres (19 miles) from central Paris, France. For Le Corbusier (1887–1965), it was the defining domestic work of his career, presented in one of his books alongside images of the Parthenon and a Bugatti sports car. There Le Corbusier noted: 'Site: magnificent property formed by a large pasture and an orchard forming a dome, surrounded by a belt of tall trees. The house does not need to have a front. Situated at the top of the dome, it must open out to the four horizons. The main level, with its suspended garden, will be elevated on piloti so that it can offer long views of the horizon.'

The house was designed as a sequence of ramps and stairs, intended to give visitors a sense of movement. Arrival was by the Savoye's chauffeured limousine, which parked inside a glass-enclosed structure on the ground floor, directly beneath the main living spaces that were planned around the open garden terrace. Visitors would disembark and proceed up through the house on a series of ramps that led by stages to the open rooftop. The house reflects Le Corbusier's ongoing obsessions: ramps, pilotis, strip windows. These were the motifs that fuelled the work of his followers around the world. Later, Le Corbusier would explore other themes and rougher materials. The villa's relationship with the landscape and the subtle precision of its geometry have led to comparison with Palladio's villas, but the floor plans, aligned for views and natural light, are less symmetrical.

Le Corbusier's foes – and there are many who blame him for the failed utopias of the 1960s – seized on the technical shortcomings that blighted the construction of the villa: walls cracked and leaked, and windows did not fit at first. However, the villa is now a protected monument, open to the public, and a reflection of the poetic possibilities of modernism.

If modernism in German architecture was shaped by the austerity of Gropius's Bauhaus, Le Corbusier's series of interwar villas had a more lyrical quality. The Villa Savoye was the most complex and most fully realized of them.

MAISON DE VERRE
Paris

1932
Pierre Chareau and
Bernard Bijvoet

Sited at the end of a quiet turning on Paris's Left Bank, Pierre Chareau's masterpiece, the Maison de Verre, is an explosive vision of the aesthetic possibilities of an exposed steel structure and industrial components put to work in the domestic world. Working in collaboration with the Dutch architect Bernard Bijvoet (1889–1979) on this project – a house for a doctor and his family, and an attached surgery – Pierre Chareau (1883–1950) moved away from the French art deco tradition where he had begun. Construction was complicated because it had to be achieved without disturbing a sitting tenant who occupied part of the site. The most impressive aspect of the exterior is the glass wall facing the street – a seamless façade of dimpled glass bricks with an opaque finish.

The main living area is a double-height, single-volume space framed by steel stanchions painted rust red, with exposed rivets suggesting the Eiffel Tower or the Forth Bridge. Chareau designed every detail – the furniture, the hopper windows, the light switches and power outlets – as if the house were one extraordinarily intricate mechanism. Floors were covered in studded rubber; cabinets and tables were made from perforated steel sheets.

For many years the house remained in the ownership of the Dalsace family, who maintained the house and its contents as a single, remarkable whole. It was subsequently acquired by an American enthusiast for early French modernism.

Chareau gave the house an enigmatic street façade of dimpled glass bricks. The double-height interior space is filled with light, but is screened from prying eyes.

24

PAIMIO SANATORIUM
Paimio

1932
Alvar Aalto

The hospital as a building type has received less attention from both architects and critics than its importance should suggest. The wave of sanatoria built in the early part of the 20th century is an exception. Tuberculosis before the development of antibiotics was a growing health emergency, for which the only treatments were complete rest in surroundings with pure air and sunbathing.

Paimio Sanatorium, set in the midst of an isolated Finnish birch forest, was one of the most distinguished examples. Alvar Aalto (1898–1976) showed a sensitive, humane understanding of the physical and emotional needs of the patients who would spend many months, and even years, in the hospital's wards. Patients lived two to a room, with washing facilities designed so as not to disturb the other occupant. Rooms had easy access to extensive sun terraces on which patients spent long periods. There were communal lounge areas, furnished with the specially designed Paimio armchair, made by Aalto's company, Artek.

Aalto won the project in a competition in 1929. He used a concrete frame, a type new to Finland at the time, creating a pristine white slab that rises out of the trees like a huge ocean liner. The Sanatorium was a complete community, with accommodation for doctors and nurses, a bakery, laundry, lecture theatre and canteen housed in separate wings.

Thankfully, the threat from tuberculosis faded in the 1960s, and Paimio was turned into a general hospital. Its size and isolated position have made that use difficult, too, leaving the sanatorium as a monument to the early days of the Modern Movement – and a reminder of our vulnerability to infectious disease.

The imagery of the Sanatorium is that of an ocean liner, moored in an endless birch forest. For many of the patients, it became a permanent home.

CASA DEL FASCIO
Como

Totalitarians are generally presented as enthusiasts for the kind of bloated monumentalism that Albert Speer served up for Adolf Hitler. In fact, the connection between classical columns and fascism is much less clear cut. The Luftwaffe was happy to commission Bauhaus-trained architects to build its airbases in glass and steel; the democracies built classical buildings just like the fascist states.

In Italy, Mussolini used a rationalist form of modernism to create a series of landmark structures across the country to demonstrate the progressive qualities of his regime. His strategy was to build a Casa del Fascio in every major Italian city, serving as local party headquarters, a base for social activities and state-run welfare services, and as a kind of architectural propaganda. The most architecturally accomplished of these was designed by Giuseppe Terragni (1904–43) for the historic centre of Como, his home town in Lombardy, Italy.

Como's Casa del Fascio was planned around an internal roofed courtyard, with one mainly glass façade facing a classical theatre and a baroque cathedral. The proportions are based on a perfect square, exactly half as high as it is wide. In the post-war years, the taint of its fascist associations overshadowed the building. It was rediscovered by a generation of revisionist historians, including Reyner Banham, who saw it as the embodiment of a view of modernity that offered an alternative to the conventional Bauhaus version.

The building continues to raise troubling questions about the tension between innate architectural qualities and the uses to which buildings are put. It is now occupied by a unit of the Italian tax police.

When he designed the Casa del Fascio in his home town of Como, Giuseppe Terragni was a convinced fascist. His experiences in Mussolini's army on the Eastern Front during the Second World War changed his mind.

ROCKEFELLER CENTER COMPLEX
New York City

1939
Wallace Harrison,
Raymond Hood,
Harvey Wiley Corbett
and others

John D Rockefeller, Jr found his way into the creation of the
Rockefeller Center through a series of accidents. The idea of
assembling a site that stretched across a whole block between
Fifth Avenue and Sixth Avenue had its roots in an attempt to
build an opera house on a 12-acre plot (around 5 hectares),
mostly owned by Columbia University, in 1928.

The opera house did not materialize, but Rockefeller, who had
been one of a group of benefactors lined up to help pay for it, took
on the project. It became a property development that resulted in
the most radical innovation on the Manhattan grid since it was first
laid out. A Midtown Manhattan essentially defined by streets and
a Fifth Avenue lined by villas were transformed by the creation of a
cluster of towers of various heights around what was a new kind of
urban space for New York: a multilevel plaza.

The architectural cast involved in the project varied over the
decade that it took to realize. The constant presence was Wallace
Harrison (1895–1981), whose entire career depended on his
close relationship with the Rockefeller family. Conceived just at
the point of the Wall Street Crash and the Great Depression, the
initial architectural vision came from Raymond Hood (1881–1934),
Harvey Wiley Corbett (1873–1954) and Wallace Harrison, who
worked to provide an overall concept to what would eventually
become nine buildings of various scales, grouped around the
Radio City Music Hall and a retail mall.

The development became one of the most successful pieces
of urbanism in New York. With its limestone skin and characteristic
setbacks, the RCA Building (now known as the GE Building) that
forms its centrepiece defined the skyscraper of the 1930s as much
as the Chrysler and the Empire State Buildings. It was here that a
famous collision between art and politics took place. The Mexican
painter Diego Rivera refused to alter the revolutionary message in
the mural commissioned from him by Nelson Rockefeller and saw
his work defaced.

The definitive image of the
glamour of the skyscraper,
the Rockefeller Center
became an archetype,
even though it was shaped
primarily by technicalities,
lift overruns and floor-area
ratios rather than aesthetics.

PALACE OF THE SOVIETS
Moscow

1941
(conceived, uncompleted)
Boris Iofan

If 'Tatlin's Tower' was a monument to Lenin, Iofan's Palace of the Soviets was intended as a gigantic celebration of Stalinism.

In 1931 Stalin selected a site, close to the Kremlin wall, for a monumental series of conference halls and meeting rooms that he planned as the symbolic centre of world communism. The site, however, was occupied by the Cathedral of Christ the Saviour – the largest Orthodox Christian church in the world – built to celebrate Russia's victory over Napoleon. Undaunted, Stalin promptly ordered the destruction of the cathedral.

An international competition was staged, open to all Soviet architects, with a number of overseas competitors, including Le Corbusier and Walter Gropius, invited to take part. In the end, the victor was Boris Iofan (1891–1976) – after the personal intervention of Stalin. Iofan was an architect recently returned from Rome, where he had practised in the studio of one of Mussolini's city planners, and very likely a KGB agent. His initial scheme was relatively restrained but, at the urging of Stalin, he inflated it to a monstrous scale. In its final form it would have been the tallest building in the world, a kind of Empire State, topped by an outsize representation of Lenin in the manner of the Statue of Liberty.

Images of the structure became a key element of Soviet propaganda, a demonstration of what Stalin could do. By the time the German invasion of 1941 stopped work, construction had reached as far as the ninth floor. The steel structure was dismantled and recycled to make tank traps. Work restarted fitfully after the war but was finally halted by Stalin's successor, Nikita Khrushchev. He had the foundations turned into a giant outdoor public swimming pool. This, in turn, was destroyed soon after the Soviet system itself collapsed by the Mayor of Moscow, Yuri Luzhkov, who raised money from the newly enriched oligarchs to fund the reconstruction of the cathedral that Stalin had destroyed.

For more than a decade, the Soviet Union was filled with stirring images of the Palace of the Soviets as it would be when finally completed, a Vatican for Stalinism, rising over the Moskva River. It was never completed.

LUIS BARRAGÁN HOUSE AND STUDIO
Mexico City

Luis Barragán (1902–88) trained as an engineer and turned to architecture only after he had graduated. His early buildings, in his home city of Guadalajara, reflected little of the qualities that would emerge in his mature work. Initially developing real-estate projects of little formal ambition in his home state, he subsequently moved to Mexico City and then to Europe, where his outlook underwent a transformation. He met Le Corbusier and became interested in his purist work. He also took inspiration from avant-garde landscape design. After he returned to Mexico, he built a modest number of private houses from the 1940s onward – including one for his own use – as well as a nunnery, a riding stable and a number of civic spaces and monuments.

All these buildings share a painterly quality: colour was very important to Barragán. He managed to achieve a synthesis between the rational geometry of the Modern Movement and a sensibility for the elements of Mexico's traditions, both pre-Colombian and colonial. In his 'blind courtyards' that capture the sky in their walls, and in his staircases free of the constraints of handrails, he offered a powerful reflection on the qualities of Mexican culture.

Barragán was ready to work as much as an artist as an architect and always insisted on extreme precision. Regarding one of his last projects, the Gilardi House (1977), in Mexico City, his client recalled how the architect had insisted on the demolition of an internal wall and rebuilding it just a few centimetres away, in the interests of getting the proportions he wanted.

Right: Luis Barragán's work in Mexico was one of the early examples of leadership in architectural culture shifting away from Europe and the United States.

Below: Barragán created a unique synthesis of the purist geometry of the European modernists and a sensibility derived from the context of Mexico.

EAMES HOUSE
Los Angeles

John Entenza, publisher of *Arts & Architecture Magazine*, initiated the Case Study programme in 1945, in an attempt to give Los Angeles a model for what modest, affordable, contemporary housing might be like. Each of the nine realized houses was documented, published and opened to the public, as a kind of outdoor exhibition, before being sold.

Set in a lush meadow overlooking the ocean, the steel-framed Eames House in Pacific Palisades is the most famous of the Case Study Houses, with its mix of high-ceilinged spaces, off-the-shelf industrial components, and a seductive simplicity that suggests both modernism and the shoji screen and tatami mat aesthetics of Japan. Charles Eames (1907–78) trained as an architect but, with the exception of this house, he is best known for his furniture, exhibitions and films. This was a house that became an intensely personal project, with authorship shared with his artist wife, Ray (1912–88). Its design evolved from an early scheme of 1945 to the built version of 1949.

The house was designed with two wings: one in which the Eames lived; the other, connected to it by an open patio, containing a studio and darkroom. Though the steel structural system is industrial – it took five men less than a day to raise the structure – the finished house is in truth more of a work of craft. Today the house is preserved as it was when the Eames family lived there: fresh flowers are placed in the living room, and Eames-designed toys are arranged on the lawn.

Right and below: Charles and Ray Eames, photographed in their intricately choreographed living room, which is filled with the trophies from their travels to India, and Latin America. It's a double height space, with a mezzanine floor for sleeping.

CITÉ RADIEUSE
Marseilles

Le Corbusier (1887–1965) practised architecture as though he were a religious missionary, zealously bent on changing the world, rather than as a disinterested professional. Since the 1920s he had been speculating about designing entire cities based on new ways of living. In the aftermath of the Second World War, he was commissioned by the French government to explore what were described as experiments in housing. The Cité Radieuse, or Unité d'Habitation, in Marseille is the most famous result of those experiments. Le Corbusier understood it not as a building but as a piece of urban fabric. With more than 300 apartments of various sizes, from bachelor studios to ample duplexes, it can house 1,600 people.

Le Corbusier wanted to make cities that allowed for a new, more communal way of life – he was fascinated by medieval monasteries and the communities that they had supported; these, he believed, could provide an architectural model for contemporary life. Within the Cité Radieuse, he included a hotel intended to provide space for guests of the occupants of the apartments, a roof garden, and shops and office spaces aligned on the famous 'street in the sky'. He even installed communal refrigerators. The shared facilities were important – the apartments themselves were long and narrow, with the only source of daylight coming from the glazed façades at each end. Charlotte Perriand and Jean Prouvé worked hard on the designs for the prefabricated kitchens, which were ingenious but restricted by space.

It took almost a decade to finish the building, a slab raised up on massive concrete legs resembling elephant's legs. What was planned as social housing was turned into a condominium. The poured concrete triggered the fashion for brutalism, though here the raw finishes were softened by a vivid paint scheme.

Right and below:
Le Corbusier's ideas for cities were always conceived on the largest possible scale: he wanted to build complete communities. The Marseilles block was the first that he actually realized. It was followed by similar projects in Berlin and eastern France.

HEADQUARTERS OF THE UNITED NATIONS
New York City

1952
Le Corbusier,
Oscar Niemeyer
and Wallace Harrison

John D Rockefeller brought the United Nations to New York by acquiring, and then donating, the 18 acres (around 7 hectares) of land – formerly occupied by slaughterhouses and slums – on which it was built.

The instantly recognizable outline of office slab and sculptural assembly building was designed in committee by a squabbling collection of internationally celebrated architects, from which Le Corbusier (1887–1965) emerged claiming that he had been robbed of the commission. The basic diagram of a high-rise slab with travertine side walls and curtain glazed façades is recognizably Le Corbusier's. Oscar Niemeyer (1907–2012), with whom Le Corbusier had worked on the pre-war Brazilian Ministry of Education in Rio, was responsible for turning the idea into a smoothly integrated set of buildings, while Wallace Harrison (1895–1981) – the Rockefellers' long-term preferred architect – actually built and detailed the complex.

Built in an idealistic attempt at world unity, to encourage peace and reconciliation, the UN debating chamber is now best known as the place where Nikita Khrushchev banged his shoe on his desk in 1960, in a fury with the delegates from the Philippines, and for the endless narcissistic posturing from a long line of demagogues.

A recent restoration project has not treated the curtain wall façades sympathetically.

It is the slab of the secretariat tower that is the most familiar landmark of the United Nations building, but it is the lower assembly building with its curved roof where the public drama takes place.

40

CHAPEL OF NOTRE DAME DU HAUT
Ronchamp

1954
Le Corbusier

Alain Couturier was a Dominican friar concerned at what he saw as the decline of religious art in the 20th century into kitsch. He was responsible for persuading Henri Matisse to create the stained glass, vestments and murals for a chapel at Saint-Paul-de-Vence as a demonstration of what might be achieved. He was equally convinced that, to retain its relevance in the modern world, the Catholic Church must embrace contemporary architecture. Couturier gave Le Corbusier (1887–1965) two commissions: for the Convent of Sainte-Marie de la Tourette, and for the Chapel of Notre Dame du Haut at Ronchamp.

Even to Le Corbusier's admirers – and, by the time it was completed in 1954, there were many of them – the Ronchamp chapel came as a shock. The young James Stirling, writing in the *Architectural Review*, implied that, by departing from the logic of the right angle, Le Corbusier was guilty of apostasy. With its massive expressive forms free-floating on a hilltop site, Notre Dame du Haut became as famous, and as instantly recognizable, as Frank Gehry's Guggenheim Museum in Bilbao would be half a century later. By shifting course so decisively away from the smooth, almost immaterial language of his pre-war work, as exemplified by the Villa Savoye, Le Corbusier was reinventing himself – much as Picasso did more than once in his career.

The Ronchamp chapel is a sculptural, emotionally charged experience. In place of proportional grids and modular dimensional systems, Le Corbusier was exploring complex curves that seemed to have come from the mornings he spent painting in his studio, before turning to architecture in the afternoons.

Right and below:
The definitive work of Le Corbusier's later career, the Chapel of Notre Dame du Haut is a sculptural manipulation of pure form and light. It was an assertion of the continuing part that progressive Catholics wanted to play in shaping contemporary culture.

PRUITT–IGOE
HOUSING PROJECT
St Louis

1954
(destroyed, 1972)
Minoru Yamasaki

Minoru Yamasaki (1912–86) was a Japanese-American architect two of whose most visible projects were prematurely destroyed. He designed the World Trade Center (1973) in Manhattan, and the Pruitt–Igoe public housing development in St Louis. Both projects have been erased: the World Trade Center through an act of terror, the other by a city administration that despaired of making the slab apartment blocks acceptable places to live. It was the manner of its demise that defined Pruitt–Igoe. The critic Charles Jencks started his polemical book *The Language of Post-Modern Architecture* (1977) by dating the death of modernism to the precise minute that Pruitt–Igoe was dynamited. It was, he suggested, a mercy killing, putting a movement in terminal decline out of its misery.

The effect of Jencks's words was somewhat undermined by the fact that there were suggestions that he got the time and date wrong. He also ignored two more fundamental questions: was Yamasaki actually a modernist? To judge by the neogothic filigree that adorned the World Trade Center's twin towers, probably not. And even if he were, was it not a preponderance of poor and out-of-work mothers, and absent fathers, rather than a malevolent architectural ideology, that did for Pruitt–Igoe?

Certainly, Pruitt–Igoe marked a watershed. It was the first time that such a conspicuous attempt at urban regeneration had gone so fundamentally wrong. If Jencks was inaccurate in his account of events, his emphasis on the demolition had the effect that he wanted. Modernism was in the dock.

Right, above and below: Minoru Yamasaki's vast housing project in St Louis was of a scale that Le Corbusier could only dream of. It also experienced harsh winters, and had racially segregated, disadvantaged residents and an inadequate maintenance budget.

44

SOUTHDALE CENTER
Edina

1956
Victor Gruen

Quite who designed the first shopping mall is the subject of some debate. The first modern out-of-town shopping centre is usually reckoned to be the Country Club Plaza, built in Kansas City by the developer J C Nichols in 1922 as part of a wider suburban community.

Victor Gruen (1903–80), a Viennese architect who came to the United States as a refugee in 1938, designed two of the earliest enclosed malls: the Northland Center, near Detroit, in 1954, and the Southdale Center in Edina, Minneapolis two years later. Southdale, which enclosed shopping streets to deal with Minneapolis's extremes of climate, was to serve as the prototype for countless malls that have followed. Almost always these would be bland boxes on the outside, rising out of seas of car parking, with department stores as anchor tenants at either end and increasingly elaborate interiors to attract jaded customers. The initial model was the 19th-century glass arcade of the Galleria Vittorio Emanuele II in Milan.

The spread of the mall phenomenon coincided with the decay of North American and European inner cities in the 1950s and 1960s, and may be seen as both a cause and an effect. Gruen himself disowned the malls, and their city-killing consequences, which he regarded as the unintended fallout from his work.

Gruen created a model that has come to transform the nature of cities everywhere – putting shopping streets inside a single building.

NATIONAL CONGRESS OF BRAZIL

Brasília

1958
Oscar Niemeyer

The decision to build a new capital for Brazil was the result of a campaign pledge from Juscelino Kubitschek while running for the presidency in 1956. Brasília was to be a move away from the colonial coastal cities and a symbolic part of Kubitschek's strategy to invest in the infrastructure of Brazil's undeveloped interior.

Kubitschek first worked with Oscar Niemeyer (1907–2012) in 1942 when he was still the mayor of Belo Horizonte. He relied on him to shape the new capital city, though the plan was the work of Lucio Costa. Despite its fluid lines, Costa's plan is essentially a paraphrase of a Roman city with two major axes crossing. Niemeyer took these elements and choreographed the expansive open space at the top of one axis, which symbolizes Brazil's government system in name as well as form: the 'Three Powers Plaza', as it is known, alludes to the judicial, legislative and presidential buildings that are grouped in and around it. Phalanxes of ministerial buildings define the plaza edges. To one side of it is the cathedral, and at the centre are twin office slabs, flanked by the Senate, marked by a convex dome, and the House of Representatives with a concave bowl.

For all its idealism and brio, this project, more than any other, suggested that modernism had lost touch with its social objectives. This was the monumental heart of a city, occupied by the elite, like Beijing's Forbidden City. Most of Brasília's three million people live out of sight, on the edges of the city, in ramshackle areas that quickly descend into favelas. When Brasília was built, the more puritanical modernists – the artist Max Bill for one – decried what they saw as the decadence of its decorative structural gymnastics. But today it looks even more of an achievement than when it was new.

Oscar Niemeyer organized the forms of the Brazilian parliament precisely to reflect its two-chamber government system. The members of each chamber share a tower housing their offices, which is split into two, with the House of Representatives on one side and the Chamber of Deputies on the other.

SEAGRAM BUILDING
New York City

In provocative charcoal drawings and a dazzling photomontage, Mies van der Rohe (1886–1969) first began thinking about the idea of a glass-walled tower in Berlin in the years after the First World War. He would not be the first architect to build one, however. Lever House on New York's Park Avenue was designed by Gordon Bunshaft of SOM and completed in 1952. It clearly draws on Mies's earlier work, but simplifies it. The Lever might not be as refined as the building Mies had envisaged but it became a precedent for commercial high-rise office slabs around the world.

Mies did it differently when he was commissioned by the Bronfman family, owners of the Canadian distillers Joseph E Seagram & Sons, to build their company headquarters on the other side of Park Avenue two years later. Samuel Bronfman had initially given the project to Pereira & Luckman, but changed his mind under pressure from his daughter Phyllis Lambert, who insisted on a more ambitious choice.

Partly because of the complexities of New York's plot ratio rules that restricted site coverage and height, and partly from his aesthetic convictions, Mies created a new model for urban high-rise development: a rectangular slab, set back from the street by an open plaza. In the Seagram, Mies set a standard for tower design that has never been bettered, through a meticulously considered set of proportional relationships that went as far as decreeing that window blinds could be set only in three positions: all the way down, halfway up, and all the way up.

In relation to the Seagram Building, Mies wrote: 'My idea, or better "direction", in which I go is toward a clear structure and construction – this applies not to any one problem but to all architectural problems which I approach. I am, in fact, completely opposed to the idea that a specific building should have an individual character which has been determined by the total problem which architecture must strive to solve.'

Mies van der Rohe's sense of order is reflected in every aspect of the façade of the Seagram. The bronze-finished steel beams on the exterior are decorative, but give the building its quality. Even the predetermined positions of the blinds reflect his discipline.

SOLOMON R GUGGENHEIM MUSEUM
New York City

1959
Frank Lloyd Wright

Philip Johnson, the master of the waspish remark, once described Frank Lloyd Wright (1867–1959) as the greatest American architect of the 19th century. Most likely, it was not to his face. Wright is America's 'sacred monster', a name known to those who could not identify a single other architect, celebrated on postage stamps, in the songs of Paul Simon and on the cover of *Time* magazine. Johnson was slyly suggesting that, while Wright did indeed shape much of modern America, there was something antique about his approach to architecture.

The Guggenheim was one of the most wilful of his designs. A museum organized as a spiral, with walls that lean outward and curve at the same time is an unforgiving and uncomfortable place to show art. Indeed, New York's art community was so convinced that the museum would be a disaster that Robert Motherwell, Willem de Kooning and 19 others signed a letter of protest to the Guggenheim's trustees. 'We shall be compelled to paint to suit Mr Wright's architecture,' one artist claimed.

Wright was self-absorbed enough to ignore both them and all his other critics, who included the Guggenheim's then director, James Johnson Sweeney. Wright tried to get him fired as he pushed on to complete his spiral idea, which he had been planning for decades and now finally had the chance to realize – no matter that it had originally been conceived as 'an automobile objective' and was now being pressed into service as a museum.

None of this matters now. Wright succeeded in creating one of the most loved and most recognizable buildings in the world.

Right and below:
Frank Lloyd Wright, in part the model for the individualistic architect in Ayn Rand's *The Fountainhead* (1943), knew how to play the part of the architect as heroic form-giver. He was working on the Guggenheim in New York almost until the day he died. As architectural sculpture, it is unsurpassed. As a place to show art, it has problems.

YOYOGI NATIONAL GYMNASIUM

Tokyo

1964
Kenzo Tange

The 1964 Olympic Games marked Japan's entry into the 'First World'. They were the first games to be held in Asia and saw Tokyo transformed with new elevated highways and subways. Kenzo Tange (1913–2005) was responsible for the Yoyogi National Gymnasium in Yoyogi Park, Shibuya.

Tange was one of a group of creative Japanese, in every field, from fashion to industrial design, film and architecture who came to prominence after Japan's defeat in the Second World War. It was as if a generation of talented individuals had been granted permission to express themselves, free for the first time from the conformity of an authoritarian society.

Tange suggested that it was seeing Le Corbusier's drawings for the Palace of the Soviets competition in the 1930s that made him want to become an architect. After graduating, he worked for Kunio Maekawa, who had once been an apprentice of Le Corbusier's. Tange synthesized the elements of European modernism into a building with a specifically Japanese character. (It should be added, however, that many of the European modernists had already been to Japan and found the sensibility of its traditional buildings an inspiration.)

Tange worked on a series of projects in the 1950s that reflected the nature of contemporary Japan, as a modern society, including the Hiroshima Peace Memorial Museum (1955) and Tokyo City Hall (1957), later demolished when the city administration moved into a new twin-tower complex at Shinjuku (also designed by Tange). The Yoyogi National Gymnasium, with its family of related forms, rising from a landscape of undulating roofs, was one of the most original.

In the 1960s Kenzo Tange's Olympic complex in Yoyogi Park provided one of the defining images of Japan's new status as economic and cultural power – Asia's first 'First World' nation.

THE ECONOMIST BUILDING
London

1965

Alison and
Peter Smithson

The question of how to build new buildings in old city streets was the abiding concern of the 1960s. The big gestures made by monolithic glass slabs sited on open plazas – an idea derived from Mies van der Rohe – were rarely successful. Alison (1928–93) and Peter Smithson (1923–2003) adopted another strategy for their commission to design an office building for *The Economist* weekly magazine. St James's Street, an 18th-century street lined by gentlemen's clubs, and culminating in a royal palace could not be mistaken for anything but the very heart of Establishment London.

The Smithsons once had something of a reputation as the angry young man and woman of architecture. They built high-rise social housing. The term 'brutalism', originally intended without negative connotations, hovered over them. Their work in St James's was anything but brutal. They placed three buildings of varying heights in a carefully considered relationship with one another, with their neighbours, and with the three streets that bound the site, around a raised plaza.

At street level, all three buildings are animated by public activities: shops, a restaurant (originally a bank) and a gallery. The Portland-stone façades are suave and well mannered. London was being offered a way to inject new buildings into some of its most traditionally minded streets through an architecture of substance.

Three modestly scaled towers, grouped around a courtyard, on the edge of St James's in London, were the European model for redeveloping city streets in the 1960s. With a mix of uses, and refined materials, they have lasted better than most of what was built in that decade.

CAESARS PALACE
Las Vegas

1966
Robert Venturi and
Denise Scott Brown

Robert Venturi (1925–) is sometimes described as the first architectural postmodernist. And it is true that the extension to London's National Gallery, designed with his wife and partner, Denise Scott Brown (1931–), does have the playful and promiscuous use of motifs from various moments in architectural history that were one of the distinguishing features of the movement. But Venturi's and Scott Brown's contribution is more complex than this label implies.

On the one hand, Venturi himself emerged as an architect to be reckoned with on the strength of the house that he designed for his mother in Philadelphia (Vanna Venturi House, 1964). This showed him as a leading exponent of a form of architecture that looked for richer spatial experiences than those that could be offered by the conventional logic of a modern plan. He was drawing on precedents from mannerist and classical buildings, such as split pediments and asymmetry. Even if he did not directly reproduce such features, this was seen as a transgression against the modernist aesthetic.

Equally notorious was the research work that Venturi and Scott Brown did with their students in the 'Learning from Las Vegas' project. At the time, the contemporary architecture wing of high culture regarded Las Vegas as the personification of all that was tasteless, crass and kitsch. In a deliberate provocation, they mapped the Las Vegas strip in search of the elements that made it so attractive to American mass audiences, and found what they described as a skilled use of iconography. Unlike the modernists, who made schools that looked like factories, houses that looked like factories, and churches that looked like factories, in Las Vegas they made casinos that looked like Roman palaces. Why shouldn't modern architects try to be crowd pleasers, too?

The original Caesars Palace, opened in 1966, had a relatively modest 680 rooms, compared with the 3,000 distributed around the present-day version.

58

MONTREAL BIOSPHÈRE, US PAVILION AT EXPO 67

Montreal

1967
Richard Buckminster Fuller

There was nobody else quite like Richard Buckminster Fuller (1895–1983). He was expelled from Harvard without a degree and worked – self-taught – on the edges of engineering, architecture and industrial design. For a time he ran a small-scale car-manufacturing business, an enterprise that came to an end when his creation, the three-wheeled Dymaxion (1933), was involved in a fatal accident. He built prefabricated metal houses, and he popularized the idea of geodesic structures, drawing on earlier work in Germany. He had a utopian worldview, reflected in his use of the term 'spaceship Earth'. According to Norman Foster, whom he once asked, 'How much does your building weigh?', he was an inspiring, collaborative partner.

The geodesic domes were his most conspicuous works. What fascinated Fuller about geodesic principles was the way that they could be used to cover enormous volumes, with the absolute minimum of material. The problem was how to put all that space to worthwhile use. Such forms do not naturally lend themselves to easy subdivision. Sometimes Fuller seemed to suggest that they should be used as protective shields – as in his scheme to put the whole of Manhattan under a dome. But they were certainly impressive, none more so than the 76-metre-diameter (250-ft) US pavilion at Expo 67, where impact was the point, rather than utility.

The dome survived the Expo, though subsequently its acrylic skin was consumed in a fire.

During Expo 67, Buckminster Fuller's dome was served by a monorail, obligatory signal of the future all through the 1960s. The acrylic skin was lost in a fire but the structure is still imposing.

FACULTY OF HISTORY, CAMBRIDGE UNIVERSITY
Cambridge, UK

1968
James Stirling

Sir James Stirling (1926–92), once the most celebrated post-war architect in Britain, won a competition to build the Faculty of History at Cambridge University in 1964. He took the distinctive geometry of the engineering building at Leicester University (1959) that he had designed earlier with James Gowan, and added red brick and tile to the palette. This proved to be a hugely influential mixture and became the dominant architectural language of the 1960s and 1970s.

However, the faculty was beset by technical problems. Reyner Banham writing in the *Architectural Review* in 1968 had to devote a substantial part of his appraisal to defending it against claims that the glazed reading room had a tendency to get too hot. By the 1980s matters were worse. The patent glazing was leaking; tiles and bricks were falling off. The problems were serious enough to give grounds for those Cambridge dons ideologically opposed to both architectural modernism and to the leftist attitudes within the Faculty of History itself to vote to demolish it, even though an entirely new building would have been more expensive than repairing the old one. At the last moment, Stirling rallied his supporters, and the structure is now a listed landmark.

During the debate, one opponent pressing for its demolition suggested: 'This building is like no other that I have learned to love. You come to the desk and realize that you are in an Edwardian hotel. Either you go up to your room, or pass beyond into the tea lounge, with the light coming from above, and no doubt a palm court orchestra.' The description caught Stirling's fancy. 'An apt description in a strange way,' he commented.

Cambridge's Faculty of History was a battleground in the culture wars of academic politics. For traditionalists, its harsh red engineering brick and its cascade of roof glass were as unwarranted an intrusion into the city as the left-wing ideologies of some faculty members. Multiple technical defects strengthened their arguments.

INTER-ACTION CENTRE
London

1971
(demolished)
Cedric Price

The only surviving structure of note by the English architect
Cedric Price (1934–2003) is the aviary at London Zoo that he
worked on with Lord Snowden. It is a striking work but hardly
reflects the regard in which Price is now held by younger architects
around the world. Price was an architectural irritant, dedicated to
undermining the priority of form and beauty, and insisting instead
on viewing architecture as a question of systems and ideas.
He was fond of pointing out that, given the treacle-like pace of
conventional construction methods, almost all buildings were out
of date before they were completed. In Price's mind, the solution
was not just to build faster by buying buildings as if they were
equipment off the shelf, but to consider building as a kit of parts,
capable of responding to unpredictable demands.

The closest that Price came to realizing such an idea was
the Inter-Action Centre, commissioned by community activists
with a cultural programme aimed at reaching deprived inner-city
communities. Exactly what would happen there, nobody quite
knew. But rather than design a set of spaces with optimistic
designations such as 'learning centre' or 'performance space',
Price provided the means for a building that would never be
finished, which would always be provisional.

It has been demolished, which perhaps suggests that
there were limits to its adaptability. With his commitment to
the ephemeral, however, Price would never have argued for
its protection by giving it landmark status.

If all buildings are out of date
by the time they are complete,
why would you build anything?
Cedric Price tried to provide
a building with a provisional
layout and structure that could
reinvent itself with the passing
of time.

OLYMPIC STADIUM
Munich

1972
Frei Otto and
Günter Behnisch

The Olympic Games of 1972 were overshadowed by the conflict between Palestine and Israel. The PLO invaded the athletes' village and took several Israeli athletes hostage. During a botched intervention by the German police, several Israelis were killed.

The tent-like canopies that cover the stadium – the most recognizable landmark of the Games – seem to belong to a very different version of the 1970s. They have an optimism and a sense of possibility that predates the Yom Kippur War of 1973 and the oil shock that followed when an Arab embargo on exports to the West triggered an economic crisis.

The graceful stadium roof by the German architect Frei Otto (1925–) reflects a more confident moment, as well as representing an approach to the stadium quite different from anything that had gone before, and rarely attempted subsequently. Rather than creating a heavy shell, Otto – a pioneer of lightweight structures – devised a covering that seems almost weightless. In its use of complex forms, the tent shapes anticipate the geometric explorations of the 21st century.

Frei Otto, an engineer as much as an architect, worked on the Munich project with Günter Behnisch (1922–2010). The spider-web tensile structure dramatically transformed the conventional model for stadiums that relied on massive concrete.

SYDNEY OPERA HOUSE
Sydney

1973
Jørn Utzon

Before Sydney built its opera house, Australia's leading city was Melbourne, and the country itself was regarded as a hot and dusty provincial reflection of the European roots of its colonists. As the art critic Robert Hughes pointed out, there was something fundamentally odd about a country that still referred to what was, geographically speaking, the Near North as the Far East.

It wasn't Sydney's opera house alone that changed that perception. The country was abandoning the White Australia Policy (admitting migrants from Europe but not Asia). It was developing a distinctive approach to food, wine and architecture. The opera house project – for all the bitterness that followed the resignation of Jørn Utzon (1918–2008), the untried Danish architect who unexpectedly won the competition to build it, when his work was only half complete – became the dominant image of Australia. It replaced a cluttered tangle of utilities on the waterfront with spectacular open spaces. The arrangement of the shell roofs provides a subtle, constantly changing sculptural composition that offers different perspectives from every angle.

At the time, the complexities of the structure were at the edge of the capabilities of engineers, who still relied on slide rules rather than computers to make their calculations. Utzon, on the other hand, was unwilling to compromise on his vision of a pure shell. His clients were in a hurry and pressed him to come up with a solution. Relations deteriorated to the point that Utzon threatened to leave in a bid to show how seriously he took the disagreements, but never expected that his resignation would be accepted. But it was and the project was completed by lesser talents.

Right and below:
Jørn Utzon went to great lengths to ensure that the quality of the finish on the roofs made them look their best. They are covered in huge quantities of mosaic tiles. During construction the tiles were laid on the ground in prefabricated panels, to ensure precision, and then lifted into place.

POMPIDOU CENTRE
Paris

When architecture seemed at its lowest ebb in the 1970s, the design for the Pompidou Centre by Richard Rogers (1933–) and Renzo Piano (1937–) was an unexpected injection of energy and optimism. It was Rogers's first big commission after the end of his partnership with Norman Foster, won in an open competition, and selected by a jury chaired by Jean Prouvé. The site was a run-down series of tenements on the edge of Les Halles, once the site of Paris's old market halls, which had been demolished in 1971 to make way for a bleak underground shopping mall.

Piano and Rogers's scheme was based on the idea of flexibility – a climbing frame of deep steel trusses that did away with the need for any internal walls or columns, allowing for multiple configurations. The centre has a whole range of cultural ingredients: a public library, the French national gallery of modern art, a performance space, as well as bookstores and cafés. It also offered one of the most spectacular views of Paris, from the flight of escalators that snakes its way up the exterior of the building.

With its colour-coded exposed ducts and vents, the exterior is a celebration of the machine age. Hostile critics called it an oil refinery, smuggled into the centre of the city. The visitors came pouring in and populated the public space in front of the main façade. The flexibility that Piano and Rogers built was put to the test. In its first 30 years, the building has been reorganized twice. Gae Aulenti (1927–2012) remodelled the art gallery, and Piano himself was asked to alter the circulation routes as part of a general overhaul that had the effect of cutting off free access to the escalators.

Right and below:
The Pompidou's street wall is a steel frame that supports the ducts and vents that service the building. Pipes are coded according to their function, a charming functionalist alibi for what is essentially a decorative idea.

BRION CEMETERY, SAN VITO D'ALTIVOLE

Treviso

1978
Carlo Scarpa

The tomb is perhaps the oldest architectural monument of all. However, the increasingly secular and sceptical modern age has found it more and more difficult to deal with buildings with a spiritual dimension, and, in the West at least, there is little appetite to confront the idea of mortality. This commission to create a private burial ground for the Brion family – owners of the Brionvega consumer electronics company, famous for using leading industrial designers such as Achille Castiglioni and Richard Sapper – has the power to transform that perception.

Carlo Scarpa (1906–78) was one of the great outsiders among 20th-century architects, with a fascination for the potential of craft skills to create rich, tactile architecture. During his career he designed a series of highly theatrical exhibitions and galleries that confronted historical elements with the strikingly contemporary.

Scarpa's burial ground for the Brion family is a moving assemblage of landscape, water and architecture. For such a small project it has reverberated around the world, inspiring architects to look for ways to move beyond everyday materialism.

Carlo Scarpa designed the tomb to embody the idea of time passing. The materials and forms taken by the walls are intended to weather and age.

LES ESPACES D'ABRAXAS
Marne-la-Vallée

1982
Ricardo Bofill

Les Espaces d'Abraxas is the work of Ricardo Bofill (1939–), a former hippie from Barcelona who became one of the more successful architects of the 1980s, turning out precast-concrete neoclassical social housing all over France. It forms the centrepiece for Marne-la-Vallée, one of the new towns that ring Paris. Bofill once optimistically called it an 'inhabited monument'. Les Espaces is made up of three apartment blocks, organized on an axis that runs through the site. There is a ten-storey, crescent-shaped block at one end, with cypress trees sprouting from the roof. Then comes an 18-storey, U-shaped block that has been hollowed out to create a dark, shadowy, Piranesian space crisscrossed by access bridges and staircases, while between the crescent block and the U-shaped block is a version of the Arc de Triomphe. This was the most exhibitionistic exercise of its kind, a deliberate reversal of all the tenets of modernist architecture, but built with all the techniques of industrialization. As if to taunt Bofill's critics, the streets in the complex were named for famous modernist architects.

The project was presented as a political statement: public housing, Bofill insisted, should have a monumental quality. It was an attempt to create a landmark in a featureless, urban landscape.

It is remarkable now that Ricardo Bofill was able to persuade so many French politicians to build so many apartments. The heroic palatial forms were achieved at the cost of contorted layouts and compromised natural light.

NATIONAL PARLIAMENT HOUSE
Dhaka

1982
Louis Kahn

Louis Kahn (1901–74) was originally commissioned to design
a legislative complex in 1961 by Pakistan's then president,
Ayub Khan. Bangladesh was still known as East Pakistan.
Work was interrupted by the war fought by India and Bangladesh
to evict Pakistan's troops in 1971, and was still far from complete
when Kahn died of a heart attack in New York's Pennsylvania
Station in 1974.

Kahn had been recommended for the project by one of his
former students at Yale. The parliament building itself is made
from roughly poured concrete and took its form from the most
fundamental of geometries: cubes, domes and circles.
Its dramatic qualities are emphasized by the reflecting pool out
of which it rises. The debating chamber, under a vaulted roof,
is at the centre of the main building, ringed by a soaring circulation
space. The complex also includes residential accommodation,
a hospital, offices and a mosque, mostly built in brick. Kahn's
work gave modern architecture what many believed it had lost in
the 1960s: a sense of memory, space and monumentality.

It is a project that shows how a design envisaged as a symbol
of the power of one state has become the embodiment of another.
Built by local labour, with very little in the way of high-tech
equipment, Kahn's work movingly overcomes the limitations
of budget and skill.

The builders of the
Bangladeshi parliament relied
less on technology than on
labour-intensive handwork,
but this in no way lessens the
monumentality of the project.
The flaws and imperfections
in the way that the concrete
was poured are lost in the
power of the composition.

SESC POMPÉIA
São Paolo

1982
Lina Bo Bardi

Lina Bo Bardi (1914–92) was born in Italy, studied architecture in Rome, and subsequently moved to Milan where she spent the Second World War and began writing for *Domus* magazine. In 1946, having married Pietro Bardi, she and her husband moved to Brazil where she designed their house (Casa de Vidro, 1951) in São Paolo. Her two major architectural projects were São Paolo's Museum of Art (1968), a concrete-and-glass box hoisted up on stilts to float over an open plaza, and the Pompéia Factory Leisure and Sports Centre, or SESC Pompéia.

This politically engaged mix of social, sports and cultural amenities for the city's working class was perhaps the most impressive of Bo Bardi's projects. She transformed a 19th-century factory that had once manufactured steel drums into an impressive blend of architectural imagination and social inclusion, converting a twin row of industrial sheds, neatly lined up along a central pathway, into a complex of subsidized restaurants and cafés, galleries, clinics and offices.

But what really sets this work apart from a conventional restoration project is the sports block that Bo Bardi built at one end of the site. Most of the land was unusable because of difficult ground conditions. There were just two possible patches on either side of an underground stream, hard against the old factory chimney. Neither one of them was large enough on its own. Bo Bardi hit on the idea of a stack of swimming pools and basketball courts on one side of the stream, with a tower of changing rooms on the other, linked at each level by flying bridges.

To create her design, Bo Bardi used raw concrete for both blocks. The sheer walls are pierced by distinctive petal-shaped openings – she called them 'caves'. They are permanently open to the elements so as to provide cross-ventilation, 'because I hate air conditioning as much as I hate carpets', as the architect put it.

An extraordinary mix of rough-cast concrete, whimsical window openings and social utopianism, Lina Bo Bardi's work was in sharp contrast to that of her Brazilian contemporary, Oscar Niemeyer.

HSBC MAIN BUILDING
Hong Kong

1985
Norman Foster

In the 1980s Hong Kong was Britain's last surviving substantial colony and facing up to the prospect of the coming handover to the People's Republic of China. A political agreement on the terms had yet to be drawn up. For the Hong Kong and Shanghai Bank, the colony's de facto central bank, stability and confidence in the financial markets were the first priority. These were certainly considerations at the bank when it began to consider the future of its headquarters office building overlooking the Star Ferry, the Hong Kong Club and the Former French Mission Building. A conspicuous investment in a prominent new building would certainly signal the continuing commitment of the bank to what was becoming an increasingly important market.

In 1979 the bank staged an international competition to find an architect, and chose Norman Foster (1935–). It was a bold choice. Foster would one day control a huge practice with more than a thousand architects, but in 1979 he had fewer than 30 assistants and had never built anything taller than four storeys. Foster effectively reinvented the skyscraper as a type, exposing its steel structure (clad in a fireproofed skin), placing a motorized set of mirrors on the exterior to direct sunlight down into the atrium, and creating a completely open ground floor.

The construction techniques were high-tech – complete prefabricated bathrooms, for example, were shipped in from Japan – but also nodded to traditional Chinese culture by being aligned with the landscape after consultations with a feng shui expert.

Right and below:
Norman Foster's first major building outside the UK was the launch pad for his career. It was one of the first convincing high-rises to be designed by a European architect, and took a bold new approach to the traditional layout of a tower, placing lifts at each end rather than in the hollowed-out centre.

HUMANA BUILDING
Louisville

For just under ten years in the 1980s, the American Michael Graves (1934–) was the most successful architect in the world. If Robert Venturi provided the intellectual ammunition for postmodernism, and Philip Johnson did best out of the publicity it generated, by getting himself onto the front page of *The New York Times*, it was Graves who provided the artistic impulse. Graves could draw beautifully. He had a strong sense of colour. He was interested in the subtleties of architectural precedents. He put all these together to create what was to become the basic recipe for commercial post-modernism, much as Mies van der Rohe had provided the steel-and-glass ingredients for corporate modernism.

Before it all went wrong and turned into a tired formula, the Humana Tower, an office building in Louisville, in the heart of the Midwest, summarized his approach in an undeniably charismatic way. Mies van der Rohe reduced the tower to a minimalist extrusion, apparently weightless, apparently effortless. Graves's version of a tower goes back to the art deco period of skyscrapers, and then further back. There are classical precedents for the emphasis that Graves put on the entrance, with its outsize pediment. Although a steel-frame structure carries the load, the building's stone skin appears to be massive. Its deep modelling gives the appearance of traditional construction, block sitting upon block, rather than the wafer-thin skin that it actually is.

For a moment the Humana seemed to sum up all that an up-to-date corporation could do to make a statement about itself. And then it turned into a flamboyant period piece.

Michael Graves beat Foster + Partners to win the competition to build the Humana tower. It was a modest 27 storeys but, with its red-granite skin and its street-level loggia, it was the personification of militant postmodernism.

INSTITUT DU MONDE ARABE
Paris

During the imperial presidency of François Mitterrand in the 1980s, Paris was recasting itself as the capital of Europe with an epic rebuilding programme. It involved a makeover at the Louvre, marked by I M Pei's glass-and-steel pyramid, and the construction of the Grande Arche at La Défense and a new National Library. They were called Mitterrand's *grands projets*.

This wave of building began with the Institut du Monde Arabe, built on the banks of the Seine by Jean Nouvel (1945–). The idea was to create a dialogue, not just with France's former North African colonies, but with the entire Arab world – a political as well as a cultural gesture. It was Nouvel's first project to achieve international visibility. He created a new approach for architecture in France, which was finally emerging from the long shadow of Le Corbusier.

The Institut is the product of two pure forms, a cube and a crescent, and makes very little use of colour, relying instead on white tiles and steel. What makes it stand out is the façade, which Nouvel conceived as a filigree screen, made of a grid of camera-like apertures, which respond to changing levels of daylight. As the metal leaves open and contract, they paraphrase decorative patterns derived from Islamic architecture. The roof is an open terrace with spectacular views over the Seine.

The Institut du Monde Arabe was the first of Mitterrand's *grands projets*, quickly followed by the pyramid at the Louvre and the Grande Arche at La Défense. Neither the Institut nor the Arche has aged well.

TERMINAL AT LONDON STANSTED AIRPORT
Stansted

1991
Norman Foster

For a passenger negotiating Stansted today, overwhelmed by budget airlines and inescapable retail outlets, it is hard to remember the terminal as it was when it first opened in 1991. It was the first airport that Norman Foster (1935–) designed and set him on the path to design two of the world's largest airports, in Beijing and Hong Kong. His objective was to simplify the experience of catching a plane. The theory was a single-level terminal that made every step of the journey, from pavement to aircraft door, clear and straightforward. Passengers would move from checkout counter to security to passport control with an unobstructed view of the runways and aircraft beyond.

Foster also had the idea of a roof that could filter daylight into the lofty departure hall below. He buried the air-conditioning plant, rather than placing it on the roof as had become conventional practice. Stansted's signature is the white-painted steel trees that support the roof and carry the air-conditioning outlets.

The terminal set a model for approaches to airport design that has been influential around the world. But even at the opening ceremony, which involved a dinner in the baggage hall, Foster cautioned against a commercialization of aviation that was turning terminals into shopping malls. A clear route from check-in to aircraft is the last thing that a retailer intending to ambush passengers and turn them into customers wants to see.

London's third airport was updated with Norman Foster's terminal building that has set a pattern for airports ever since. Services are moved off the roof to allow for a lightweight, pavilion structure.

GUGGENHEIM MUSEUM
Bilbao

1997
Frank Gehry

When the New York City-based Guggenheim Museum agreed to work with the Basque regional government to build a museum carrying the Guggenheim's name in Bilbao, it was a landmark in the history of museums. For perhaps the first time the idea of franchising a museum brand had taken shape. There was, of course, already a Guggenheim in Venice, but that was the product of Solomon Guggenheim's niece Peggy's independent collection that had been acquired by the Guggenheim Foundation on her death. What Bilbao's politicians wanted from the Guggenheim was a famous name and access to an impressive collection of modern art, as part of the city's multifaceted efforts at culture-led urban regeneration.

What ensured the abiding fame of the project was the titanium-clad 'train crash' of a building by the Canadian-American architect Frank Gehry (1929–), a billowing free-form sculpture on an urban scale that shocked its way onto the front page of *The New York Times* when it opened. It was the architect's masterpiece, transforming him from avant-garde outsider to mainstream icon, and in the process redefining the boundaries of contemporary architecture.

It was the first in a wave of what were called 'iconic' buildings – each attempting to outdo its predecessors – that strove to give previously obscure post-industrial cities an instantly recognizable landmark that would somehow make them register on an international scale. The boosters called it the 'Bilbao effect'. And for a while the Basque city did indeed flourish in the glow of the publicity and the tourism that the project attracted. It was not, however, simply because of one spectacular building that Bilbao's fortunes turned around. It was simply one part of a coordinated strategy that included investment in a subway system and a new airport. The subtleties were lost on countless cities that began increasingly futile attempts to ape Bilbao.

The traffic-stopping geometry of the Bilbao Guggenheim, and Gehry's selection of titanium for its skin served to create a dazzling, unforgettable image. It was exactly what the Basque government wanted.

KUNSTHAUS BREGENZ
Bregenz

1997
Peter Zumthor

Peter Zumthor (1943–) bases his architectural practice in a simple barn-like structure in a remote Swiss valley. He is careful about accepting too many projects, preferring to concentrate on making every design that his studio works on a personal project, rather than creating the larger-scale studio that would be needed to build an airport or a skyscraper. Zumthor has nevertheless attracted worldwide attention for the poetic sobriety of his work. He creates intensely considered architecture in which the emphasis is on the fundamentals of light, materials and space.

Zumthor attracted a great deal of attention for the work that he did on Therme Vals (1996), a spa complex at Vals, close to his studio, which almost resembles a shrine. A more public project is the gallery he built in Austria at Bregenz, where the emphasis was on creating a series of spaces in which the architecture all but disappears, and in which the light is modulated to make the best possible setting for looking at art.

Right and below:
Externally, the concrete structure is sheathed in glass. Inside the building, galleries are linked by staircases that are considered as the main spaces.

ABBEY OF NOVÝ DVŮR

Toužim

2002

John Pawson

The collapse of the Soviet Union transformed Central Europe's cultural landscape. In Czechoslovakia, organized religion had had a difficult time. Catholic priests were forced into marriage to avoid government sanctions.

Nový Dvůr, near Toužim in the Czech Republic, was the first new monastery to be established after the end of communism. A group of devout young men went to a French monastery to begin the process of becoming monks, with the long-term aim of establishing a new foundation in their home country. When the French abbot was convinced that the novitiates were ready, he sent them home to set about building a new monastery.

A ruined baroque manor house two hours outside Prague was donated to the order. The monks looked around for an architect and saw the secular work that the British minimalist designer John Pawson (1949–) had done. They prepared a careful brief: life for a silent order is hard enough; the architecture should not make it harder. There were to be no squeaking floorboards to disturb sleeping monks while their brethren woke throughout the night to observe the offices. The design had to acknowledge that some brothers snore.

Within the framework of the restored manor house, Pawson built a new chapel and created a cloister that reflects the ancient rule of the Cistercian order. He worked with light, artificial and natural, and with proportions, striving for the elimination of every unnecessary visual distraction.

The abbey's chapel is one of the entirely new sections. It is used throughout the day and night by the monks as they celebrate the offices prescribed by their order's rule.

KUNSTHAUS GRAZ
Graz

2003
Peter Cook and
Colin Fournier

In the 1960s Peter Cook (1936–) was a leading figure behind the establishment of Archigram. This architectural group proposed a much less doctrinaire, much lighter Anglo-Saxon version of the Futurist architecture of Antonio Sant'Elia, and its members poured more energy into an extraordinary sequence of self-generated projects characterized by startling imagery than they did into actually building anything. Among its projects was Peter Cook's own Plug-in-City (1964), which proposed a megastructure made up of standardized cells rather than buildings.

It was not until long after Archigram was dissolved that Cook got to build anything on a serious scale. The arts centre in Graz was the result of a collision between the baroque 'gingerbread' buildings of Austria and the technophilia of Cook, who here worked in collaboration with Colin Fournier (1944–). Every aspect of it – the cartoon plan, the bulbous deep-blue elements for the skin, the ranks of periscopes emerging from the roof – suggest a kind of playful anarchy. The building is like a blue submarine that has been smuggled ashore.

Right and below:
A blue glass skin wraps gallery spaces and skylights into a single voluptuous form.

SELFRIDGES
Birmingham

Jan Kaplicky (1937–2009) was born in Czechoslovakia, but left for London after the Russian invasion of 1968. He was a passionate believer in the possibilities of technology, but also a consummate creator of architectural imagery. The department store that he designed and his partner Amanda Levete (1955–) built while they practised as Future Systems was a declaration of what architecture could be.

Sitting in the middle of the everyday commercial world of central Birmingham, it looked like a startling visitation from another planet. The conventional pattern of a multistorey department store is transformed and housed inside a free-floating blob studded with aluminium discs. Kaplicky compared it to a Paco Rabanne metallic dress from the 1960s. It was a low-cost way to achieve dramatic results. Set into the disc screen are a number of windscreen-like window openings, emphasized by a vivid yellow border that oscillates with the Yves Klein-blue backdrop. At a higher level, a curving walkway from the neighbouring car park penetrates the discs.

The department store was one of the great inventions of the 19th century, almost a museum in which the newly affluent learned how to spend their wealth in ways that reflected well on them. The type almost died in the 20th century, but the work by Future Systems for Selfridges pointed to a new direction.

PHAENO SCIENCE CENTRE
Wolfsburg

2005
Zaha Hadid

Wolfsburg is the German city built by Volkswagen. One half is an industrial complex of power stations and factories dedicated to turning out cars on production lines. The other half of the city is a civic centre, with a concert hall designed by Alvar Aalto and a range of public buildings. The Phaeno Science Centre by Zaha Hadid (1950–) is positioned on the boundary between the two halves of the city. It is both a piece of architecture and an element that forms part of the landscape.

Hadid's design lifts the building up on a set of concrete legs that open up the ground as a public space. She merges urbanism and building, blending the ground into walls and floors and roof. The building itself is a series of intersecting planes, into which has been injected a whole series of exhibits aimed at providing young people with an understanding of the principles of science.

The geometry of the steel-framed roof is a tour de force of design by the engineers Karim Taylor, and for once is left visible – in her later buildings Hadid has always hidden the sinews that make her work possible.

Right and below:
Wolfsburg is a company town – it exists to build Volkswagen cars. But over the years it has acquired a cultural hinterland. Aalto built there. Zaha Hadid's science centre is at the edge of Wolfburg's industrial heart and its civic core.

CCTV HQ
Beijing

When Rem Koolhaas (1944–), the most acerbic architectural thinker of his generation, was selected to design the headquarters of Central China Television (CCTV), his critics suggested that, while it might be acceptable for liberal-minded Western architects to construct hospitals or even airports in China, for them to design a landmark for one of the principal propaganda organs of a repressive regime was more questionable. Koolhaas shrugged off such suggestions as 'somehow ornamental': how could one not take part in the greatest single wave of construction that the world had ever seen?

In fact, the CCTV HQ building has had a troubled history for other reasons. The Communist Party leadership took some convincing that such an apparently outlandish design was appropriate. For Koolhaas, it was an answer to the question of how do you make a landmark in the midst of a forest of new towers each clamouring for attention. You don't try to be the tallest or the most imposing at all. Instead, you play a different game, by different rules. Koolhaas suggested that he had folded a tower as tall as the World Trade Center into a more complex version of the high-rise.

The CCTV HQ offers a wide range of different types of space at different levels, offices as well as studios, and both public and private areas. And it is also a clearly distinctive silhouette on the horizon, marked by the engineer Cecil Balmond's seemingly random pattern of creases on the glass skin that are the traces of steel bracing, organized at points of maximum stress rather than to a visually coherent pattern. The building's impact was marred by official Chinese disapproval when a fire broke out during an unauthorized firework display, causing unknown loss of life.

The meaning of the new headquarters of China's broadcasting organ was hotly contested. Critics saw it as the centre of a repressive regime's propaganda activities; Koolhaas as a chance to take part in the modernization of the world's most populous state.

NATIONAL STADIUM
Beijing

2008
Herzog and
de Meuron

Jacques Herzog (1950–) and Pierre de Meuron (1950–), Basel-based architects who have worked together since they were at school, gained their international reputation for their transformation of London's old Bankside power station into the new Tate Modern. It gave them the opportunity to work on larger and larger landmark-scale projects, of which the National Stadium, built for the 2008 Beijing Olympics, was perhaps the most visible. China saw the Games as a chance to mark its coming of age as a global superpower, no longer the dusty hermit kingdom of the Mao years.

Herzog and de Meuron worked with the Chinese artist Ai Weiwei (1956–) to create a concept for the project. Their idea was quickly nicknamed the 'Bird's Nest', but the most impressive achievement in Beijing was that the stadium – typically conceived as a simple container – was transformed into a public arena that encompassed a series of interstitial spaces, between the outer shell of the building and the auditorium itself.

For China, this was a key project in the West–East transfer of technology. The complex steel structure was made in China, but the skills that made it possible were down to the involvement of Western experts.

Right and below:
Like Koolhaas's CCTV landmark, the National Stadium was created to reflect a newly powerful China.

NEUES MUSEUM
Berlin

2009
David Chipperfield
Architects

The destruction of Berlin at the end of the Second World War, and its subsequent partition into eastern and western halves, set the scene for an important assessment of the nature of architectural memory and reconstruction.

The museum itself was built in the days of the Prussian construction of Germany, and it was a civic landmark to give the newly emerging state an archaeological collection. It was designed by Friedrich August Stüler (1800–1865), a student of Karl Friedrich Schinkel, the architect of the Altes Museum, which stands immediately adjacent. In the last days of the Nazi regime, the ceremonial centre of Berlin, of which the Neues Museum is a part, was seized by the Russians and the museum's collections were scattered.

The museum was left a roofless ruin, pockmarked by shells. Rebuilding did not start for 60 years, until the Cold War came to an end and Germany was reunited. The office of the British architect David Chipperfield (1953–) won the competition to restore the ruin to its original use as an archaeological museum. Chipperfield's strategy was regarded as radical in the extreme, not because he wanted to introduce a bold new work, but because he kept the old fragments of the original building visible – the pockmarks and the decay, the patched repairs, and the traces of the themed decoration from the museum's earliest incarnation – and complemented them with new additional structures to give back order and completeness to the building.

For Chipperfield, leaving the marks of time passing was not only a more intellectually coherent approach; it also offered a rich aesthetic experience, and the Neues Museum was re-established in form and figure as a contemporary building.

Right and below:
David Chipperfield's work
with the Neues Museum
set out to reconcile two
very different views of
Berlin's history.

NATIONAL MUSEUM OF AFRICAN AMERICAN HISTORY AND CULTURE

Washington, DC

2016
(projected)
David Adjaye

David Adjaye (1966–), the Tanzanian-born, London-based architect of Ghanaian origin, working with a team of American firms as the Freelon Adjaye Bond / Smithgroup, has built on the last vacant site on Washingon's Mall, otherwise lined with a ponderous file of officially sanctioned cultural institutions. These go from the 1940s classicism of the National Gallery, with I M Pei's limestone-prism extension, to the 19th-century gothic of the Smithsonian, and Gordon Bunshaft's corporate modernism at the Hirshhorn.

The newly created institution, officially titled the Smithsonian National Museum of African American History and Culture looks very different from them. It is positioned at the very heart of the US capital, at the edge of the Washington Monument. The task facing Adjaye was complex: to respond to the L'Enfant Plan from 1791 on which Washington is based, to relate to the architectural expression of its neighbours, but also to create a clear statement of African Americans' place in their country.

Due to open in 2016, the museum comprises 30,000 square metres (323,000 sq. ft), rising five floors over a substantial underground presence. Adjaye has reflected African American traditions in the bronze filigree screen in which the design wraps the above-ground part of the building, in its relationship with the landscape, through what he calls a 'porch', and in the form of what he calls the 'corona', the above-ground expression of the building.

David Adjaye is the lead designer of the National Museum of African American History and Culture, with the Freelon Group as architects of record. It stands on the last remaining vacant site at the heart of Washington, next to the Washington Monument.

INDEX

PICTURE CREDITS

CREDITS

An Hachette UK Company
www.hachette.co.uk

First published in
Great Britain in 2015
by Conran Octopus,
a division of Octopus
Publishing Group Ltd
Endeavour House,
189 Shaftesbury Avenue
London WC2H 8JY
www.octopusbooks.co.uk
www.octopusbooksusa.com

Copyright © Octopus
Publishing Group Ltd 2015

Distributed in the US by
Hachette Book Group
1290 Avenue of the
Americas, 4th and 5th Floors,
New York, NY 10020

Distributed in Canada by
Canadian Manda Group
664 Annette St., Toronto,
Ontario, Canada M6S 2C8

A CIP catalogue record for
this book is available from
the British Library.

Text written by:
Deyan Sudjic

Commissioning Editor:
Joe Cottington
Senior Editor:
Sybella Stephens
Copy Editor:
Robert Anderson
Design:
Untitled
Picture Research Manager:
Giulia Hetherington
Senior Production Manager:
Katherine Hockley

Printed and bound in China
10 9 8 7 6 5 4 3 2 1

ISBN 978 1 84091 680 5